DARJEELING
TRAVEL GUIDE 2025

Your Passport to Exploring
Darjeeling's Hidden Treasures
and Scenic Wonders in 2025

Jimmy Britt

COPYRIGHT © 2024 BY JIMMY BRITT

TABLE OF CONTENTS

CHAPTER ONE: WELCOME TO DARJEELING

A thriving hill town known for its stunning scenery, rich cultural legacy, and internationally recognized tea estates, Darjeeling is tucked away in the eastern Himalayan foothills. This picturesque town in West Bengal, known as the "Queen of the Hills," is a captivating fusion of tranquil scenery, colonial-era beauty, and a distinctive combination of Tibetan, Indian, and Nepalese traditions. Darjeeling provides activities that enthrall tourists all year long, regardless of whether they are adventure seekers, tea connoisseurs, or nature lovers. Everything you need to know for a successful trip to this Indian treasure is included in this book.

The Essence of Darjeeling

1. A View of the Peaks

The vista of Mount Kanchenjunga, the third-highest peak in the world, is among Darjeeling's most famous attractions. From the Tiger Hill vantage point, it is breathtaking to watch the dawn over these snow-capped peaks as the first rays of sunshine illuminate the mountains in shades of pink and gold. Photographers and tourists alike are drawn to Darjeeling's panoramic vistas from many locations, such as Batasia Loop and Observatory Hill.

2. History and Tradition

The colonial past of Darjeeling is deeply ingrained in its history and is reflected in its architecture. The town gracefully maintains its colonial past, from British-style mansions to historic sites like the Darjeeling Himalayan Railway (a UNESCO World Heritage Site). The "Toy Train," which was first operated in the 19th century, continues to chug over hills and tea plantations, offering tourists a picturesque and sentimental experience.

3. The Tea Gardens of Fame

Darjeeling produces some of the best teas in the world, making it a household name. Visitors are drawn to its verdant tea gardens, such as those at the Makaibari and Happy Valley estates. You may learn about the production, processing, and tasting of tea by taking a guided tour of these estates. Darjeeling tea is widely valued across the globe because of its unique musky-sweet scent and delicate taste, which are present in every cup.

4. Mosaic of Culture

As varied as its terrain, Darjeeling's culture is shaped by Bengali, Tibetan, and Nepali populations. This blending of cultures is reflected in the local festivals, dancing, music, and cuisine. An authentic cultural experience is provided by the area's Buddhist monasteries, Hindu temples, and Gorkha influences. Visitors may see local customs during the yearly Durga Puja, Losar (Tibetan New Year), and other festivities.

5. There's Adventure Ahead

In terms of outdoor activities, Darjeeling is a paradise for adventure seekers. The town provides a range of exhilarating adventures, from rock climbing at Tenzing Rock to hiking and camping in the neighboring Singalila National Park. A well-liked option, the Sandakphu Trek leads hikers along paths that provide breathtaking views of Makalu, Lhotse, Kanchenjunga, and Mount Everest. Other thrilling activities that make Darjeeling a great place for explorers include paragliding and river rafting on the Teesta River.

Planning Your Trip

1. Traveling by Air: Bagdogra Airport, which is around 70 kilometers distant, is the closest airport to Darjeeling. Major cities like Delhi, Guwahati, and Kolkata provide direct flights. You may rent a private vehicle or take a cab from Bagdogra to Darjeeling in around three hours.

By Rail: The nearest significant train station that links Darjeeling to other Indian cities is New Jalpaiguri (NJP). You may either take a cab from NJP or board the Toy Train of the Darjeeling Himalayan Railway, which provides beautiful vistas and takes around seven hours to get to Darjeeling.

By Road: Darjeeling has excellent road access to neighboring cities and towns. From Siliguri or Gangtok, you may take a shared Jeep, a cab, or a private vehicle.

2. Places to Stay

Darjeeling has a variety of lodging options, ranging from colonial-style hotels and opulent resorts to affordable guesthouses and homestays. Historic establishments such as the Windamere Hotel and Glenburn Tea Estate provide sweeping mountain vistas and an air of the past. Guesthouses in neighborhoods like Chowrasta and Gandhi Road are popular choices for tourists on a tight budget. During busy times, reservations should be made in advance.

3. Local Transit

The easiest modes of transportation in Darjeeling are shared cabs and Jeeps. You may also rent a bike rickshaw or walk lesser distances. Darjeeling's winding, narrow roads may be difficult to maneuver; thus, using local transportation is preferable to driving. Riding the Darjeeling Himalayan Railway to see neighboring communities and sites is another exceptional experience.

4. Regional Food

The cuisine of Darjeeling is a delicious fusion of Bengali, Nepali, and Tibetan flavors. You must try traditional foods like churpee (hardened cheese), thukpa (noodle soup), and momos (dumplings).

Along with Tibetan specialties like gyathuk, Nepali foods like sel roti and gundruk are also well liked. The ideal location for tea lovers to have a genuine Darjeeling tea experience is Glenary's or Nathmull's Tea Room.

Best Times to Visit

1. Spring (March to April): With bright skies and temperatures between 8°C and 15°C (46°F and 59°F), spring is one of the most picturesque seasons to visit Darjeeling. As orchids, magnolias, and rhododendrons blossom, the hills become a vibrant canvas.

Activities: Trekking, sightseeing, and seeing tea farms are all excellent in the spring. It's the perfect time of year for photography because of the beautiful weather and new flowers. In the nearby woodlands, birdwatchers may also see a range of local and migratory species.

2. Summer (May to June): Weather: With pleasant temperatures ranging from 11°C to 19°C (52°F to 66°F), summer is the busiest travel season. Darjeeling is still colder than other Indian cities, even if it is milder than other seasons.

Activities: Trekking, going to Tiger Hill to see the dawn, and taking part in local festivities are all great throughout the summer. It's the perfect time of year to explore tea gardens and take beautiful train trips because of the pleasant weather. However, reservations for lodging and excursions should be made in advance owing to the high demand at this time of year.

3. Monsoon (July to September): The monsoon season is characterized by high rainfall and temperatures between 13°C and 18°C (55°F and 64°F). Road closures and landslides often occur, making travel more difficult.

Activities: Although the monsoon season brings with it verdant scenery, it is not the best time of year for outdoor pursuits. However, it's a more sedate time of year with fewer visitors for those who want to see Darjeeling's tranquil side. Museum tours and tea tastings are excellent examples of indoor attractions.

4. Autumn (October to November): Clear skies, comfortable temperatures (around 10°C to 16°C or 50°F to 61°F), and breathtaking mountain vistas make this a great time of year to visit.

Activities: Hiking, touring, and taking in the joyous atmosphere of regional festivals like Dasain and Diwali are all best done at this time of year. With its vivid autumn foliage and pristine vistas of Kanchenjunga, photography is also a pleasurable experience.

5. Winter (December to February): Weather: Darjeeling has chilly winters, with nighttime lows of 2°C (36°F) and daily highs of 8°C to 12°C (46°F to 54°F). At higher elevations, snowfall sometimes falls, giving the scenery a mystical feel.

Activities: For those who like the cool, crisp air and a less crowded experience, winter is ideal. Cozy lodgings provide warmth and relaxation after touring, and hot tea is particularly soothing in the cold weather. The tea estates and vantage points around Darjeeling also have a special attraction because of the winter scenery.

Last Words of Advice for Your Darjeeling Journey

Clothes: Wear layers since the temperature might change over the day. It's wise to have a lightweight jacket on hand for the cold mornings and nights, even throughout the summer.

Altitude Adjustment: Due to Darjeeling's height, some tourists may have moderate cases of altitude sickness. The transition may be facilitated by drinking plenty of water and avoiding strenuous activity during the first several days.

Responsible Tourism: Traditional populations and delicate ecosystems may be found in Darjeeling. Bring reusable bags and water bottles to reduce waste and show consideration for regional traditions.

Darjeeling is a place that captivates tourists with its stunning scenery, diverse culture, and kind locals. Every visitor may have a wonderful time at this hill station, whether they are taking a picturesque trek or enjoying a cup of delicious Darjeeling tea while taking in the valley views. Make a good travel plan, choose the ideal time of year, and see the beauties of this Himalayan gem.

CHAPTER TWO: GETTING TO KNOW DARJEELING

History and Cultural Heritage

Darjeeling has a distinct identity within India because of its history, which is entwined with Tibetan influences, British colonialism, and Gorkha culture. The Lepchas, the local indigenous population, lived in the area when it was a part of the Kingdom of Sikkim. Before the British East India Company took over in the 1830s, it was occupied by the Gorkhas from Nepal in the beginning of the 19th century. Darjeeling's milder temperature and expansive Himalayan vistas made it an attractive hill station hideaway to the British.

The first tea estates were founded in 1841, and Darjeeling tea quickly became well-known around the world for its subtle taste and fragrance. Nepali workers were drawn to Darjeeling's tea plantations, resulting in a blending of local and Nepali culture that is still noticeable today. The Darjeeling Himalayan Railway, which connected the town to the lowlands and promoted commerce and tourism, was finished in 1881. The economics and accessibility of Darjeeling were significantly shaped by this "Toy Train," which is now a UNESCO World Heritage Site.

Due to the unique cultural and linguistic identity of the Nepali-speaking community, the Gorkhaland movement—a call for a separate state—rose to prominence in Darjeeling after independence. The movement created the semi-autonomous Darjeeling Gorkha Hill Council, which gives the area greater authority over local administration even though Darjeeling is still a part of West Bengal.

A varied blend of Christian, Buddhist, and Hindu customs defines the region's cultural legacy. Churches, monasteries, and temples coexist; both residents and visitors are drawn to famous sites like the Mahakal Temple, the Japanese Peace Pagoda, and the Dhirdham Temple. In addition to the British colonial architecture seen in churches, homes, and schools, festivals like Losar, Dasain, and Tihar display a fusion of Nepali, Tibetan, and Indian elements.

Climate and Weather Patterns

The climate in Darjeeling is often categorized as subtropical highland, with notable seasonal variations in temperature and precipitation.

1. March through April is spring.

With its pleasant temperatures and minimal humidity, spring is one of Darjeeling's most picturesque seasons. On the slopes, flowers such as orchids, magnolias, and rhododendrons bloom during the 8°C to 15°C (46°F to 59°F) daytime temperatures. With sunny skies and pleasant temperatures, this time of year is perfect for hiking and sightseeing. During this season, the well-known Darjeeling Orchid Festival often takes place, drawing both plant lovers and photographers.

2. May through June is summer.

In comparison to the rest of India, the summers are moderate, with average highs of 11°C to 19°C (52°F to 66°F). Even if the afternoons can grow a little warmer, the weather is still cold and comfortable. The town might become congested at the busiest times of the year, but the pleasant weather makes it possible to do things like hike, take a tea garden tour, and see Tiger Hill at dawn. As the monsoon draws near, the humidity begins to increase, but it is still tolerable, so it's a nice time to go outside.

3. July to September is monsoon season.

Darjeeling has intense rains during the monsoon season, when average temperatures range from 13°C to 18°C (55°F to 64°F). The wettest months are July and August, and landslides are frequent, interfering with outdoor activities and transportation. The village goes through a calmer phase as fewer visitors come, even if the verdant surroundings are a visual feast. The monsoon season offers a more sedate, mist-filled atmosphere for those looking for a tranquil getaway. However, owing to the possibility of travel delays and slick roads, prudence is suggested.

4. fall (October to November)

With cool, clean air and temperatures between 10°C and 16°C (50°F and 61°F), autumn is another ideal season. Beautiful views of Mount Kanchenjunga and other peaks are possible due to the often clear sky. The post-monsoon foliage gives the scenery more vitality, and the weather is perfect for hiking. Fall is also festival season, with holidays like Diwali and Durga Puja bringing joy to the area.

5. December through February is winter.

Winters are chilly, with daily highs of 8°C to 12°C (46°F to 54°F) and nightly lows sometimes falling to around 2°C (36°F). Although it may happen at higher elevations, snowfall is uncommon in Darjeeling town proper. For those who like cool, crisp air and the allure of foggy mornings, winter is the best time of year since it is calmer. With tea pluckers harvesting in the chilly air, the area's tea plantations are particularly lovely during this season. Temperatures might drop, so it's important to have warm clothes with you.

Language, People, and Local Customs

1. Language

Given the sizeable Nepali population, Nepali is the most common language spoken in Darjeeling. Hindi and Bengali are also extensively spoken and understood, particularly in tourist destinations and marketplaces. Because of the impact of British missionaries who founded a number of educational institutions in the region, English is widely used in hotels, shops, and schools. While knowing a few Nepali words, such as "Namaste" (Hello), might be a polite gesture while conversing with locals, travelers just need a basic understanding of Hindi or English to go about the area.

2. Individuals and Ethnicity

In addition to a modest Bengali community, the majority of the people living in Darjeeling are Nepalis (Gorkhas), Lepchas, and Bhutias. The biggest group is made up of Gorkhas, who have a distinct cultural identity shaped by Buddhist and Hindu customs. The indigenous Lepcha people of Darjeeling have a unique language and culture that is based on ancient animistic beliefs and nature worship. The Tibetan Buddhist traditions and practices have been perpetuated by the Bhutias, who are originally from Tibet.

In Darjeeling, where different religious and cultural customs coexist, the variety of these cultures has produced a distinctive social fabric. The region's festivals, cuisine, music, and fashion all reflect its culture. Traditional clothing is still worn, especially during festivals and festivities, such as the gunyu cholo worn by Nepali women and the daura suruwal worn by Nepali men. Darjeeling residents are renowned for their friendliness and kindness, which makes visitors feel at home.

3. Spirituality and Religion

Christianity, Buddhism, and Hinduism are all practiced in Darjeeling. There is a notable presence of Hinduism, which is mostly embraced by the Bengali and Nepali minorities. Important structures include the Mahakal Temple atop Observatory Hill. With monasteries like the Yiga Choling Monastery (Ghoom Monastery) acting as spiritual hubs, Buddhism, which is connected to the Bhutia and Tibetan populations, is also very important. British missionaries brought Christianity to the area, and there are a number of churches from the colonial period there, including St. Andrew's Church.

The culture of Darjeeling is characterized by the harmonious coexistence of various faiths. Both residents and visitors often visit temples and monasteries, which provide a glimpse into the spiritual life of the area. The town's cultural liveliness is enhanced by the enthusiastic celebration of religious holidays including Dasain, Tihar, Losar, and Christmas.

4. Etiquette and Local Customs
The culture of Darjeeling is strongly rooted in reverence for elders and sacred sites. Basic politeness is demanded of visitors, including modest clothing and taking off shoes before entering temples or monasteries. Being kind and considerate is appreciated while engaging with locals. Basic

pleasantries like "Namaste" or "Tashi Delek," a Tibetan welcome, are appreciated by the typically hospitable inhabitants of Darjeeling.

Sharing a cup of Darjeeling tea is a customary act of hospitality, and tea is an essential component of social life. Accepting a cup of tea when asked to a local's house is considered courteous since refusing might be seen as rude. Although it's typically OK to take photographs, it's polite to get permission before doing so, particularly when photographing individuals or places of worship.

5. Customary Dance, Music, and Festivals

Dance and music are fundamental to the cultural expression of Darjeeling. The ethnic variety of the area is reflected in traditional dances like the "Tamang Selo" and folk melodies like the "Bhanu Sangeet." Locals dress traditionally and perform during festivals, which turn into a vibrant event.

Folk music often uses the "madal," a native Nepali drum.

Communities in Darjeeling come together during festivals, which infuse the area with color and vitality. Important Hindu holidays, Dasain and Tihar, are extensively observed, with marigolds and oil lamps adorning dwellings. Another important celebration is Losar, the Tibetan New Year, which is celebrated with masked dances, prayer services in monasteries, and vibrant decorations.

The region's cultural legacy is promoted via the annual Darjeeling Carnival in November, which features local talent in dance, music, and the arts. Tourists may feel Darjeeling's sense of togetherness and cultural pride during this festive time.

The allure of Darjeeling is found in its rich cultural heritage, picturesque scenery, and friendly locals. Travelers' experiences are enhanced when they are aware of its history, climate, and subtle cultural aspects; this allows them to immerse themselves in a dynamic cultural tapestry rather than merely enjoy a picturesque getaway. With this knowledge, tourists may experience Darjeeling in its authentic form and establish a connection with the local customs, history, and people.

CHAPTER THREE: WHERE TO STAY

Top Hotels and Resorts

1. Darjeeling's Mayfair

Mayfair Darjeeling provides comfort, elegance, and colonial beauty in a prominent position with stunning views of the Kanchenjunga range. This historic hotel offers spa services, well-furnished rooms with contemporary conveniences, and beautifully planted grounds. Premium accommodations and lavish suites are available, and visitors may take advantage of the beautiful settings, luxurious furnishings, and attentive service. There is a bar, a multi-cuisine restaurant, and a health spa among the amenities.

2. Darjeeling's Elgin

The Elgin, a historic royal home with British colonial architecture, is well-known for its antique appeal. The rooms are tastefully equipped with vintage furniture, classic fireplaces, and opulent facilities, creating an old-world vibe. This historic hotel has lounge spaces, an on-site spa, and a restaurant open all day. It is well located for both shopping and tourism, close to Mall Road.

3. Hotel Windamere

The 19th-century Windamere is a historic property that appeals to those who value a traditional setting. Known as a history hotel, it is situated on Observatory Hill and offers breathtaking views. An authentic colonial experience is provided by the distinctive design of each room, which includes historical furniture. A library, a comfortable dining area, and a beautiful setting for classic afternoon tea are among the amenities. The hotel's rich history is its hallmark experience, offering candlelight meals and a distinctive sense of British tradition.

4. The Cedar Inn

The opulent Cedar Inn hotel offers expansive views of the valley below and the mountains from its hilltop location. It blends traditional Tibetan elements with modern design. The rooms are roomy and have lovely views of the surroundings. A spa, a fitness center, and an outdoor terrace with a fantastic view of Kanchenjunga are among the amenities. In a warm, welcoming setting, the on-site restaurant offers a variety of cuisines, including continental and local delicacies.

5. The Spa and Resort at Central Heritage

Located in the center of Darjeeling, this 4-star resort provides contemporary lodging with a touch of traditional design. The resort is perfect for families and couples since it offers luxurious rooms and suites with all the facilities you need. Key attractions are easily accessible due to its central position. A multi-cuisine restaurant, a bar, a wellness spa, and a kid-friendly indoor play area are among the amenities. It is a practical and pleasurable option, and guests like the personal service and cozy atmosphere.

Budget-Friendly Accommodations

1. Zambala Spa and Retreat

Zambala Retreat provides reasonably priced lodging with nice facilities, such as tastefully decorated rooms and contemporary restrooms. With accommodations that are roomy, tidy, and affordable, the hideaway offers a cozy atmosphere. It is well situated for those seeking convenience and a tranquil setting, close to the Darjeeling train station. Delicious Indian and Tibetan food is served at the on-site restaurant, and there are also some basic spa services offered.

2. Seven Seventeen Hotel

Hotel Seven Seventeen is a popular low-cost choice in Darjeeling that blends contemporary conveniences with a traditional Tibetan atmosphere. The rooms are comfortable and reasonably priced, with minimal amenities and décor with Tibetan influences. The hotel has a restaurant serving Indian and Tibetan food and a small gift store selling handicrafts from the area. It's a great starting point for touring since it's near Mall Road, and both families and travelers adore the kind staff.

3. Everest Villa

Villa Everest offers a tranquil, cozy stay at a fair price, situated a little away from the bustling neighborhoods. Spacious rooms with traditional décor and views of the green surroundings may be found on this lovely property. In addition to enjoying the calm setting away from the bustle of the city, visitors may have prepared meals at the hotel's on-site restaurant. For tourists looking for a low-cost getaway, Villa Everest provides a peaceful environment.

4. Mohit Hotel

The Hotel Mohit provides reasonably priced, well-appointed rooms and excellent services. Basic facilities like TV, Wi-Fi, and private toilets are included in the roomy, tidy accommodations. It is in a handy position, close to shopping and activities. Indian, Chinese, and regional cuisine are served in the hotel's on-site restaurant. It is an affordable choice for tourists seeking simple amenities and a convenient location since it also has a modest patio with picturesque views.

5. Spa and Golden Dolma

Golden Dolma and Spa, which is close to Chowrasta, offers reasonably priced accommodations with decent amenities. The facility has a spa that provides affordable relaxing treatments, and the rooms are comfortable and furnished with necessities. A range of regional and North Indian cuisine is served in the hotel's restaurant. It is a good option for tourists on a tight budget seeking convenience because of its convenient location and reasonable cost.

Unique Stays: Tea Estates and Boutique Lodges

1. The Tea Estate & Boutique Hotel Glenburn

One of Darjeeling's most well-known lodging options is Glenburn Tea Estate, which gives visitors the opportunity to spend time on a functioning tea farm. Situated just outside of Darjeeling, this opulent estate offers roomy apartments with private verandas, antique décor, and breathtaking views of the river valleys and mountains. Visitors may take a tour of the tea estate, sample tea, and relax in the lovely gardens. For a full experience, hikes and riverside picnics are planned, and gourmet dinners are offered in the dining area. For those looking for a calm, immersing vacation into Darjeeling's tea culture, Glenburn is the perfect place.

2. The Tea Retreat at Tumsong

This boutique hotel is tucked away in the Tumsong Tea Estate, between tea farms and scenic surroundings. The rooms are large, traditionally decorated, and have balconies with wonderful views of the mountains. Visitors may visit the tea factory, take guided tours of the tea gardens, and see how tea is made. The retreat is the perfect retreat for eco-tourists and those interested in learning about Darjeeling's tea business since it provides meals that are obtained locally, an outdoor sitting space, and a tranquil ambiance.

3. Chiabari Mountain Retreat & Spa in Chamong

This hideaway, which combines luxury and nature, is situated inside the Chamong Tea Estate. Visitors are accommodated in tasteful, cozy rooms with expansive windows overlooking the tea plantations and mountains. Bird viewing, woodland hikes, and tea garden excursions are among the activities offered at Chamong Chiabari. Additionally, the resort provides health programs and a spa with Ayurvedic therapies. Couples and families seeking an opulent vacation in nature will find it perfect due to its serene location, opulent facilities, and emphasis on relaxation.

4. Singtom Resort & Tea Estate

Another distinctive tea estate lodging option is Singtom, which combines boutique resort amenities with historic charm. For those who want to experience a more genuine tea estate without leaving Darjeeling town, this property is perfect. The estate provides extensive tea excursions, tastings, and plantation walks, and the rooms are furnished with antiques. Singtom offers a distinctive, opulent substitute for conventional hotels with individualized service, locally produced cuisine, and a focus on environmentally responsible methods.

5. The Tea Estate bungalow

The Bungalow by the Tea Estate provides a homey experience on a tea plantation for those looking for seclusion and quiet. Individual cottages with rustic décor, contemporary conveniences, and a warm, inviting ambiance are available at this boutique hotel. Visitors may unwind in a natural environment away from the bustle of the city, tour the neighboring tea gardens, and sip freshly brewed tea. Families or groups seeking a quiet, independent retreat with the allure of rural Darjeeling would love this choice.

Advice for selecting lodging in Darjeeling

Location: Because Mall Road and Chowrasta are adjacent to important landmarks, retail establishments, and dining options, these neighborhoods are the best choices for convenience. However, a peaceful experience in stunning natural settings may be found at tea plantations and boutique lodges beyond the main town.

The facilities offered by Darjeeling's lodgings range from modest, reasonably priced alternatives to opulent hotels with spas, excellent cuisine, and planned activities. Choose the services and degree of comfort you want.

Experiences: Staying on a tea plantation offers a unique viewpoint and immersive experiences like tea tours and tastings for those who are interested in the tea culture. While bigger hotels may have planned sightseeing and adventure activities, boutique lodges provide cozy, rural settings.

Peak Season Considerations: Spring (March to April) and fall (October to November) are the busiest travel seasons in Darjeeling. It is advised to make reservations in advance during certain periods since accommodations tend to fill up rapidly.

Darjeeling has a range of lodging options to suit all price ranges. While budget hotels provide minimal comfort and are often in a central location, luxury hotels and resorts offer all the facilities and picturesque vistas. Although the cost of tea estates and boutique lodges varies, they often provide a mid-range to premium experience with a distinct appeal.

Accessibility: Verify the lodgings' ease of access, particularly if you want to walk or have mobility issues, since some are situated on slopes or just outside the main town. Hotels around Mall Road are often closer to important attractions and easier to get to.

Weather Preparedness: The weather in Darjeeling may be erratic, particularly from June to September when it rains a lot. When making reservations, take into account that certain tea plantation lodgings could not be accessible during periods of intense rain, particularly if your trip falls during the rainy season.

Make reservations in advance: Darjeeling sees a spike in visitors during holiday seasons like Christmas and Diwali. It is strongly advised to make reservations in advance during certain periods, particularly if you want to stay at one of the tea plantations or boutique hotels, which sometimes have a limited number of rooms.

Darjeeling has something for every kind of tourist, whether they are looking for an opulent getaway with views of the mountains, an affordable location with easy access, or an unusual stay on a functioning tea farm. The area's many lodging options, which range from luxurious hotels to quaint lodges and picturesque tea farms, let you experience Darjeeling's splendor in comfort and elegance.

CHAPTER FOUR: EXPLORING SCENIC WONDERS

Majestic Mountain Views

With the magnificent Kanchenjunga, the third-highest peak in the world, taking center stage, Darjeeling provides some of India's most spectacular mountain vistas. Kanchenjunga, sometimes called the "Sleeping Buddha" because it resembles a reclining figure, is visible from many locations in Darjeeling, particularly at dawn when the snowy peak is illuminated by the sun's golden colors.

1. The Tiger Hill

The most well-known spot in Darjeeling for morning views of Kanchenjunga and, on a clear day, Mount Everest is Tiger Hill. It takes an early start and is around 11 kilometers from the major town, but the experience is definitely worth it. To guarantee a location and see the first rays of sunrise turning the pink peaks into brilliant orange, visitors often come before morning. Tiger Hill's viewing platforms can hold sizable crowds, but getting there early guarantees a decent view. Even though it may become rather cold in the winter, vision is improved by the clean, fresh air.

2. The Loop of Batasia

With its planted garden and spiral train track, the Batasia Loop provides sweeping vistas of the surrounding valleys and mountains. The Kanchenjunga range serves as the background for this picturesque location, which is 5 kilometers from Darjeeling and a station on the Darjeeling Himalayan Railway (Toy Train). The Batasia Loop's appeal as a picturesque and historic location is further enhanced by the Gorkha War Memorial, which honors Gorkha troops, and by offering a tranquil setting for leisurely strolls amid vibrant flower beds.

3. The Hill of Observatory

Situated in the center of Darjeeling, Observatory Hill offers breathtaking mountain vistas and the ancient Mahakal Temple, which is devoted to Lord Shiva. It is well-liked by both residents and tourists because of its spiritual vitality and natural beauty. Prayer flags blow in the wind around the temple, giving the distant vista of Kanchenjunga a mysterious feel. Especially at dawn and sunset, this spot is perfect for a more tranquil experience since it is less busy than Tiger Hill.

4. The Sandakphu Peak

The highest mountain in West Bengal, Sandakphu, provides an unmatched perspective of the Kanchenjunga range's "Sleeping Buddha" creation for those who are ready to go beyond. It is around 58 kilometers away from Darjeeling and may be accessed by four-wheel drive or a multi-day hike. The distinctive feature of Sandakphu is that, on a clear day, it provides views of four of the five tallest peaks in the world: Everest, Kanchenjunga, Lhotse, and Makalu. Trekkers and anyone seeking a high-altitude experience will love this vantage point.

Iconic Tea Plantations

With estates producing some of the most valuable teas in the world, Darjeeling is well known for its tea. Rich soil, altitude, and a chilly temperature make it possible to grow tea with a distinctive taste. In addition to being a sensory experience, visiting these tea plantations offers the chance to take in Darjeeling's stunning scenery and tea-making legacy.

1. Tea Estate in Happy Valley

Happy Valley, one of Darjeeling's oldest tea farms, was founded in 1854 and is just 3 kilometers from the town. The plantation, which is well-known for its picturesque vistas and guided tours, lets guests stroll through tea gardens, see the plucking process, and discover how a leaf becomes a cup. The tour guides at the estate share their knowledge of traditional tea-processing techniques and the elements that contribute to the subtle scent of Darjeeling tea. Additionally, the farm has a tasting area where guests may buy fresh tea packets straight from the plantation and experience several tea kinds.

2. The Tea Estate at Glenburn

About an hour's drive from Darjeeling, Glenburn Tea Estate provides a luxurious experience among verdant tea farms. Visitors may stay in an estate-style cottage at Glenburn, which was founded in 1859 by a Scottish tea firm, and experience life on a tea plantation. The fields, tea processing facilities, and tasting sessions are all included in guided tours that highlight the production of oolong, green, and black teas. The estate, which is situated on hillsides with a view of the Rangit River, offers a tranquil haven with breathtaking views that go beyond tea production to include outdoor pursuits like birdwatching, fishing, and nature hikes.

3. The Tea Estate of Makaibari

Makaibari Tea Estate in Kurseong, 32 kilometers from Darjeeling, is well-known for being among the first tea plantations worldwide to use organic and biodynamic growing methods. It is a must-see for tourists who care about the environment. It was founded in 1859 and produces premium teas, such as Silver Tips Imperial, which is only collected on full moon evenings. Makaibari's dedication to fair trade, community welfare, and sustainable farming is highlighted on guided tours. In addition, the estate provides lodging opportunities so that guests may enjoy the hospitality of the locals while seeing the factory and tea gardens.

4. Darjeeling's Organic Tea Gardens

Organic tea plantations that emphasize environmental sustainability and provide tours to highlight environmentally friendly tea manufacturing have become more prevalent in Darjeeling in recent years. Organic farming is the main emphasis of gardens like Ambootia and Selimbong, which produce premium teas while protecting the surrounding environment. In addition to offering visitors the opportunity to participate in plucking sessions that combine conventional and organic techniques, these estates often host courses on sustainable farming. Walking through the rows of tea plants around picturesque mountains is a rejuvenating haven for nature enthusiasts, and the mood in these gardens is serene.

Hiking Trails and Nature Walks

Trekkers and environment lovers find refuge in Darjeeling's varied terrain, which includes hills, forests, and streams. Darjeeling offers a variety of hiking and wildlife routes, from short strolls for novices to strenuous expeditions for experienced explorers. Every route provides a different perspective of the Himalayas, native plants and animals, and an opportunity to fully appreciate the area's natural splendor.

1. The trek to Singalila Ridge

The Singalila Ridge trip, one of the most well-known in the area, begins at Manebhanjan, around 26 kilometers from Darjeeling, and winds through Singalila National Park. Known for its expansive vistas of Mount Everest and Kanchenjunga, this 80-kilometer journey takes four to five days to complete. The walk winds through thick bamboo, magnolia, and rhododendron woods, where visitors may see Himalayan black bears and red pandas. Along the way, trekkers may stay in charming mountain lodges where they can experience the local way of life while taking in the breathtaking mountain scenery.

2. Trails in Tinchuley and Lamahatta Villages

The Tinchuley and Lamahatta paths combine nature, culture, and visual splendor for those looking for a shorter, less demanding excursion. About 25 kilometers from Darjeeling, Tinchuley offers treks through tiny villages, tea estates, and pine woods. In contrast, Lamahatta has well-kept eco-parks with picturesque views and bamboo forests. Families and nature enthusiasts seeking a leisurely trek will adore these pathways. Homestays are available in Tinchuley and Lamahatta, enabling guests to experience the warmth of the locals while taking in the serene landscape.

3. The Sandakphu Trek

Often referred to as the "trekker's paradise," the Sandakphu trek is a strenuous but worthwhile journey that begins in Manebhanjan and covers around 31 kilometers. West Bengal's highest mountain is Sandakphu, and the path provides unparalleled vistas of four of the top five summits in the globe. The hike travels through Singalila National Park, which has vistas of the majestic Himalayas, dreamy valleys, and thriving rhododendron woods. Between April and May, or October and November, when the weather is clear and the flowers are in bloom, is the ideal time of year to hike Sandakphu.

4. Trails in Senchal Wildlife Sanctuary

There are a number of quick and simple nature paths through thick woods in the Senchal Wildlife Sanctuary, which is close to Tiger Hill. The sanctuary, which spans 40 square kilometers, is home to a variety of plants and animals, such as sal trees, oaks, and orchids, as well as creatures like leopards and barking deer. The sanctuary's trails provide a peaceful respite from the hustle and bustle of the metropolis and are perfect for photography, nature hikes, and bird watching. Senchal Lake and the far-off Himalayan peaks are visible to visitors, making it a fantastic day trip destination from Darjeeling.

5. The Ridge Walks at Kurseong and Mahaldiram

About 30 kilometers from Darjeeling, Mahaldiram and Kurseong provide picturesque ridge treks with breath-taking vistas of the far-off mountains, valleys, and tea estates. These routes provide a more private experience since they are less crowded with visitors and are moderately strenuous, requiring two to three hours to finish. Particularly well-known for its stunning dawn views and opportunities to see uncommon birds like the red-billed blue magpie and Himalayan bulbul is the Kurseong Ridge Walk.

Travelers may extend their trip by discovering Darjeeling's scenic treasures, which include its breathtaking mountain vistas, famous tea farms, and immersive hiking routes. By showcasing the area's unmatched beauty and cultural value, each of these natural sites enables tourists to establish a connection with the local environment and inhabitants. Darjeeling's timeless appeal and natural majesty are revealed at every turn, whether you're walking up the Singalila Ridge, exploring organic tea farms, or taking in the view of Kanchenjunga from Tiger Hill.

CHAPTER FIVE: MUST-SEE ATTRACTIONS

Tiger Hill Sunrise

Tiger Hill, which lies around 11 kilometers from Darjeeling town, is well-known for its morning views of the third-highest mountain in the world, Kanchenjunga. This 2,590-meter (8,497-foot) viewpoint is popular with both residents and tourists because it provides an amazing perspective. In order to see the sun gently rising over the Himalayan range, people go to the peak in the early hours before dawn.

Why It's Unique

The visual drama that develops as the sun rises is what makes Tiger Hill so magical. The snow-capped summits are given a dreamlike glow as Kanchenjunga first glows pink before becoming dazzling gold. You could even get a distant view of

Mount Everest on clear days. When visibility is at its optimum, which is between October and December and March and April, this celestial sight attracts large people.

Tips for Visitors

Arrive early, preferably before 4:30 AM, to experience Tiger Hill to the fullest, particularly during the busiest travel seasons. Due to the restricted area at the viewpoint, a good viewing place is guaranteed if you start early. Wearing thick layers is crucial since winter mornings may be quite cold. The majority of tourists plan their transportation from Darjeeling the night before, and shared Jeeps are a well-liked and affordable choice.

Other nearby attractions

Many tourists continue their day by touring neighboring locations after dawn. Near Tiger Hill lies the Senchal Wildlife Sanctuary, which has natural pathways ideal for leisurely walks through oak and pine woods. The Yiga Choeling Monastery in Ghoom, which is well-known for its exquisite statue of Maitreya Buddha and old Buddhist scriptures, is another well-liked choice.

Darjeeling Himalayan Railway

Known affectionately as the "Toy Train," the Darjeeling Himalayan Railway is one of India's oldest mountain railroads and a UNESCO World Heritage Site. This narrow-gauge railway, which was built in 1881, was designed to traverse the rough terrain between New Jalpaiguri and Darjeeling, a distance of around 88 kilometers. The train's recognizable steam engines and picturesque route have come to represent the history and allure of Darjeeling.

Historical Importance

The railway was constructed to make Darjeeling, a British hill station at the time, more accessible. The train can climb more than 2,000 meters because of its creative design, which incorporates loops, reverses, and grades. In addition to being a means of transportation, it is now a historical landmark that takes visitors back in time while providing information about colonial engineering and the particular difficulties of constructing a railway in the Himalayas.

Paths and Encounters

The Joy Ride, which travels the picturesque Batasia Loop from Darjeeling to Ghoom in two hours, is the most well-liked excursion. Passengers are treated to expansive vistas of Kanchenjunga and the valleys below as the train winds its way around this loop. The nostalgic feeling is enhanced by the Ghoom Museum near Ghoom station, which displays vintage photos, genuine tools, and memorabilia.

The train also makes journeys between New Jalpaiguri and Darjeeling for people who want a longer journey. The whole trip, which winds through towns, woods, and tea plantations, takes almost seven hours. Passengers get a close-up look at the area's natural beauty and traditional way of life via this immersive experience.

Reservations and Useful Information

Booking in advance is advised due to the Toy Train's enormous popularity, particularly during the busiest travel seasons (April–June and October–December). The Indian Railways website and regional travel firms both sell tickets. Steam and diesel engine choices are available, and the Joy Ride leaves many times daily. In order to guarantee a seat on the steam-powered coaches, which are especially popular with photographers and aficionados, reservations should be made well in advance.

Possibilities for Photography

From the lively streets of Darjeeling town to the verdant tea plantations and untamed mountain scenery along the route, the Darjeeling Himalayan Railway provides an abundance of photographic opportunity. With its floral gardens, war monument, and expansive vista of the Himalayan range, the Batasia Loop is very picturesque. Take a trip in the morning or late afternoon when the sun is shining on the scenery for the best light.

Padmaja Naidu Himalayan Zoological Park

The Darjeeling Zoo, sometimes called Padmaja Naidu Himalayan Zoological Park, is home to a wide variety of high-altitude animal species, many of which are indigenous to the Himalayas. The tallest zoo in India, spanning 67.5 acres and concentrating on the protection of endangered animals, is situated at an elevation of 2,134 meters (7,000 feet).

Famous Locals

The zoo is well known for its conservation and breeding initiatives, especially for Himalayan wolves, snow leopards, and red pandas. One of the zoo's main attractions is the red panda, a famous representation of the eastern Himalayas. The cages at the zoo are designed to resemble the animals' natural habitats so that guests may see them in conditions that are comparable to those in which they would naturally live.

The zoo is home to red pandas as well as the elusive and uncommon snow leopard, which is hard to see in the wild. The Padmaja Naidu Himalayan Zoological Park is one of the few locations on Earth where tourists may get a close-up look at this amazing predator. Siberian tigers, clouded leopards, and Asiatic black bears are among the other creatures that support the zoo's dedication to the protection of high-altitude species.

Institute of Himalayan Mountaineering
Dedicated to teaching climbing, the Himalayan Climbing Institute (HMI) is located on the zoo's

grounds. The institution was established in honor of Tenzing Norgay, who ascended Mount Everest with Edmund Hillary in 1953. It provides Himalayan mountaineering-related seminars, exhibitions, and equipment displays.

Norgay's accomplishments and a variety of mountaineering relics, like original equipment from earlier trips, are on display at HMI's museum. The museum provides a valuable perspective on the difficulties experienced by early mountaineers and is a great addition for anybody interested in Himalayan adventure.

Tips for Visitors

There is a lot to see and learn at the zoo and HMI, so allow at least half a day to explore both thoroughly. Given that the zoo's terrain may sometimes be steep, comfortable walking shoes are advised. The zoo's natural location gives it the perfect place to take pictures of animals and beautiful scenery, and photography is permitted. Families and parties can unwind with ease thanks to the on-site café, which serves light fare.

Programs for Education and Conservation

The zoo conducts a number of conservation and educational activities, including endangered species breeding programs, research projects, and animal preservation awareness campaigns. Zoo guides may provide informative tours for visitors, including details on the diets, habits, and conservation status of the animals. In order to promote a greater awareness of animal protection, the zoo also offers programs for kids during the busiest travel seasons.

Tickets and Accessibility

The zoo is open from 8:30 AM to 4:30 PM every day except Thursdays; the exact hours may change somewhat depending on the season. Visitors may easily tour both the zoo and the Himalayan Mountaineering Institute since tickets cover both.

From Darjeeling town, Padmaja Naidu Himalayan Zoological Park is conveniently accessible by taxi or shared jeep. For milder weather and fewer visitors, it is best to go there early in the morning.

In conclusion, Darjeeling's natural beauty, cultural legacy, and dedication to conservation are all encapsulated in these three must-see sights. While the Darjeeling Himalayan Railway takes tourists through beautiful scenery and history, Tiger Hill provides a dawn experience that will never be forgotten. Lastly, the inspirational heritage of the Himalayan Mountaineering Institute serves as the background for Padmaja Naidu Himalayan Zoological Park, which exposes tourists to the uncommon and endangered animals of the area. When combined, they provide a thorough overview of the distinctive features that make Darjeeling a popular Himalayan trip.

CHAPTER SIX: HIDDEN GEMS OF DARJEELING

Local Markets and Artisanal Crafts

You may discover the town's distinctive fusion of Himalayan culture, local crafts, and traditional cuisines at Darjeeling's bustling local markets. Several smaller, lesser-known locations provide a more personal look into local life and handcrafted items, even though visitors often congregate at the bigger markets.

Busty Market in Bhutia

Known for its genuine Tibetan handicrafts and antiquities, this bazaar is a hidden gem close to the Bhutia Busty Monastery. Silver, turquoise, and coral jewelry, woolen shawls, and elaborately carved wooden sculptures are among the goods sold by the vendors here. This market is perfect for discovering one-of-a-kind, handcrafted goods that showcase the town's rich cultural past since it is more subdued and focuses on local crafts.

Bazaar Teesta

Teesta Bazaar, which is just a short drive from Darjeeling town, focuses on traditional commodities and artisanal crafts, particularly those produced from bamboo and cane. Everything from unique bamboo souvenirs to handmade furniture and baskets may be found here. Locally cultivated medicinal herbs that are offered by herbalists who may provide information about their health advantages are another reason for this market's popularity. Teesta Bazaar is a local favorite and provides a genuine feeling of Darjeeling's artisanal traditions, despite being tiny and off the usual route.

The Chowk Bazaar

Chowk Bazaar is a hidden treasure for those who are ready to investigate, while being well-known among residents and less well-known to visitors. The market has kiosks selling Tibetan carpets, handcrafted textiles, and traditional attire like the chuba, in addition to fresh fruit and street cuisine. This is the perfect place for foodies to try Tibetan bread, momos, and thukpa, a noodle soup that is a mainstay of the local cuisine.

Lesser-Known Temples and Monasteries

Even though Darjeeling is home to several well-known religious locations, a number of less-traveled temples and monasteries provide a more serene, contemplative setting. These locations are significant both culturally and spiritually, demonstrating the region's distinctive blend of Buddhist, Hindu, and Buddhist traditions.

Eco Park and Monastery in Lamahatta

Lamahatta Eco Park, a secret haven of peace and spirituality, is located around 23 kilometers from Darjeeling. The park, which is surrounded by thick pine trees and has a view of the magnificent Himalayan range, has a number of nature paths that end in a tiny, remote monastery. Few visitors visit this serene monastery, which makes it the ideal place for introspection. In addition, the environmental park has a holy pond, several picturesque vantage spots, and lovely prayer flags.

Monastery of Dali

A short drive from Darjeeling town lies the lesser-known Dali Monastery, also called Druk Sangag Choling Monastery. The monastery, which is home to over 300 monks, is part of the Tibetan Buddhist Drukpa Kagyu tradition. The expansive complex has vibrant murals, exquisitely painted walls, and a large prayer hall embellished with traditional Buddhist artwork. The monastery offers guests a very spiritual experience in the early morning hours when the sound of singing monks fills the air.

Temple of Mahakal

Mahakal Temple is well-known in the area, although fewer visitors visit it because of its rather obscure position atop Observatory Hill. This temple is special because it combines Buddhism with Hinduism, drawing both Buddhist monks and Hindu followers. It has a view of Kanchenjunga in the distance and is encircled by old trees and flying prayer flags. According to legend, this temple was transformed from a Buddhist shrine to a Hindu one centuries ago, symbolizing the peaceful coexistence of the two faiths in Darjeeling.

Secret Viewpoints and Serene Spots

There are several well-known vistas in Darjeeling, but the more subdued ones let tourists appreciate the peaceful beauty of the town. These undiscovered locations provide serene backdrops for photography, introspection, or just a simple getaway into nature, making them perfect for anybody looking for expansive views away from the throng.

Lepchajagat Point of View

Lepchajagat, a tiny town and wildlife reserve with stunning views of Kanchenjunga and the surrounding woods, is located around 15 kilometers from Darjeeling. Though less well-known, this viewpoint provides a calm, unobstructed vista of the Himalayan range. The mist rising from the valleys below makes for very lovely mornings. Lepchajagat is the perfect location for a peaceful dawn or sunset, as there aren't many tourists there. There are hiking paths in the vicinity where you may see local wildlife and plants.

Tinchuley

About 32 kilometers from Darjeeling, this little, unusual settlement provides some of the nicest, lesser-known vistas of the Teesta Valley and Kanchenjunga. "Tinchuley" means "three chimneys," alluding to the three notable hilltops that form the background of the settlement. In addition to providing beautiful walking routes through tea plantations and orange orchards, it's a great place to go bird watching. Tinchuley is a peaceful haven for those wishing to take in Darjeeling's natural splendor away from the throngs of visitors since it is still mostly uninhabited.

Tea Estate Rangli Rangliot

Rangli Rangliot is a hidden treasure renowned for its remote location and extensive history, even though many people visit the more well-known tea farms. This tea plantation, which means "this place of our own," provides expansive vistas of tea gardens against the striking background of Kanchenjunga. In contrast to more commercial farms, Rangli Rangliot offers a peaceful setting where guests may stroll around the gardens, learn about the tea-making process, and taste some of the estate's best teas. This estate makes it possible to experience Darjeeling's tea culture in more intimacy since there are fewer tourists.

Ridge of Sandakphu

Despite being a popular destination for trekkers, fewer people go to Sandakphu to reach its viewpoints, which provide unmatched 360-degree views of four of the five tallest peaks in the world: Makalu, Kanchenjunga, Everest, and Lhotse. The highest peak in West Bengal, at 3,636 meters above sea level, provides unparalleled sweeping vistas. From Manebhanjan, Sandakphu is accessible via a strenuous jeep ride or a multi-day hike. With its picturesque woodlands, rhododendron blossoms, and far-off mountain views, the drive itself is a fulfilling experience. This crest provides some of the most breathtaking views of the Himalayas for those who are able to walk.

These undiscovered Darjeeling treasures emphasize the area's rich culture, profound spirituality, and stunning scenery while providing experiences that go beyond the typical tourist trappings. Visitors may experience the genuine character of the town more intimately at these locations, which range from the artisan marketplaces where traditional crafts are preserved to the serene monasteries that provide spiritual comfort and the hidden vantage points that showcase Darjeeling's natural splendor. For those seeking a more intimate, calmer trip into the heart of Darjeeling, each of these jewels rewards a longer examination.

CHAPTER SEVEN: FOOD AND DINING

Traditional Darjeeling Cuisine

With traditional tastes from Bengali, Tibetan, and Nepalese culinary traditions, Darjeeling's food reflects its many cultural influences. A range of vegetables, meats, and dairy items are paired with strong, earthy spices in these dishes, which are often made using fresh local ingredients. A variety of filling stews, dumplings, and rice-based dishes are typical meals.

Momos

Momos, Tibetan-style dumplings stuffed with minced meat or veggies and served steamed or fried, are a mainstay in Darjeeling. Before being filled with vegetables like cabbage, onions, and carrots or meats like beef, pig, or chicken, the dough is often hand-rolled and formed into tiny dumplings.

71

Momos are a must-try, traditionally served with a fiery tomato chutney.

The Thukpa

Originating in Tibet, this hearty noodles soup is a favorite among Darjeeling residents and tourists. A mix of veggies or meat, including beef or chicken, a mild broth, and freshly prepared noodles make up this dish. Ginger, garlic, green chilies, and other spices are used to flavor thakpa, a hearty and tasty soup that is ideal for the chilly mountain environment.

Sinki and Gundruk

Popular in Darjeeling, gundruk and sinki are distinctive fermented vegetable dishes that are essential to Nepali cuisine. Radish roots are fermented to make sinki, while leafy greens are fermented to make gundruk. The resultant earthy and tangy pickled tastes give rice or curry dishes a taste boost. These foods have a powerful, unique flavor and are high in probiotics.

Rice flour is used to make Sel Roti, a Nepalese sweet bread that is deep-fried into a ring form. It is often consumed at festivals and other special events because it is soft on the inside and slightly sweet and crispy on the exterior. Sel roti is a popular breakfast or snack food that is often enjoyed with a hot cup of tea.

Combination of Aloo Dum with Sel Roti

Alai dum with sel roti is a common street food combination that combines the sweetness of sel roti with spicy, slow-cooked potatoes. A tasty meal with a hint of heat is produced by cooking the potatoes in a rich tomato-based stew with spices including chili powder, cumin, and turmeric.

The Phagshapa

A Sikkimese and Tibetan specialty, this pig dish is especially well-liked in Darjeeling during the winter months. For a fiery and smokey taste, pagshapa is made of strips of pork belly fried with radish and dried chilies, seasoned with ginger and garlic. The beef becomes juicy and soft from the lengthy cooking procedure, making the meal substantial and satisfying.

Best Restaurants and Cafes

There are several cafés and restaurants in Darjeeling that serve both foreign and traditional local cuisine, so there's something for everyone. These restaurants, which often have breathtaking views of the surrounding mountains, provide atmosphere and authenticity.

Glenary's

Since more than a century ago, Glenary's has been a staple of Darjeeling's eating scene. Pasta, pizzas, and delectable baked goods are among the restaurant's

Western and Indian specialties, but it's most known for its bakery. The café area is perfect for sipping Darjeeling's renowned tea with a freshly baked pastry because of its antique décor and Himalayan outlook.

Restaurant Kunga

Tibetan and Nepali cuisine are the specialties of this welcoming, family-run eatery. Thukpa, phing (glass noodles), and Tibetan-style meat meals are among the traditional foods that may be sampled at Kunga, which is well-known for its substantial portions and genuine tastes. It is a well-liked option for both residents and tourists due to its compact size and cozy ambiance.

Sonam's Kitchen

Sonam's Kitchen, a tiny, friendly restaurant with a large following, is well-known for its breakfast selections, including pancakes, eggs, and toast with handmade preserves. The café's welcoming ambiance and plenty of vegetarian alternatives make it popular among tourists looking for comfort cuisine with a regional flair.

Keventer's

An iconic Darjeeling landmark, Keventer's is well-known for its English-style breakfasts. The café is well-known for its rooftop seating, where you can have their famous breakfast platters—which include eggs, bacon, and sausages—while taking in views of the Alps. In addition, they provide burgers, sandwiches, and milkshakes.

The revolver

A hidden treasure in Darjeeling is this café with a Beatles motif. Revolver is well-known for its delectable and reasonably priced Naga cuisine, like smoked pig and fiery chutneys, in addition to its unique décor. With Beatles memorabilia decorating the walls, the atmosphere is warm and nostalgic, making it a special place to dine.

The Park Eatery

The Park provides a variety of cuisines in a welcoming setting for individuals who want to try Chinese and Indian food. This restaurant is well-known for its classic Indian curries and Thai-style dishes. It's a terrific choice for a leisurely lunch after a day of touring because of its welcoming decor and helpful personnel.

Street Food and Local Eateries

The street food scene in Darjeeling is a lively medley of tastes, with vendors serving light fare that reflects the region's many culinary traditions. A must-do activity for tourists visiting Darjeeling is sampling street food, which gives them a taste of genuine regional cuisine at reasonable costs.

Locals love Kwati, a filling stew cooked from a variety of nine sprouting beans, particularly in the rainy season. When khati is cooked with garlic, ginger, turmeric, and chile, it creates a tasty, nourishing soup that is comforting and satisfying. It's ideal for a light lunch or fast snack, and street sellers often serve it in little bowls.

Aloo Dum

Boiled potatoes are cooked in a thick, spiced tomato stew to make aloo dum, a spicy potato dish that is a mainstay of Darjeeling's street food scene. It is often served by vendors with puris or sel roti, which gives the dish a chewy, filling texture. For those who want to sample real Darjeeling tastes, this meal is perfect since it is tasty and a little spicy.

Shaphaley

A Tibetan delicacy called shaphaley is made of dough that has been filled with spices, minced meat, and cabbage, folded into a half-moon shape, and deep-fried till golden crisp. Shaphaley is served with spicy chutney by street sellers. It is a well-liked choice for a fast and tasty nibble because of the mix of the crispy bread and rich filling.

Churpee

Churpee, a kind of hardened cheese produced from yak or cow milk, is a distinctive food that is often offered by neighborhood sellers. It is rich and chewy, with a hint of saltiness. Both soft and hard variants of churpee are available; the tougher ones are eaten as a snack and provide a distinctive gastronomic experience for daring diners.

Soup with Mulligatawny

Mulligatawny soup, a South Indian-inspired meal with a regional touch, is cooked with lentils, veggies, and coconut milk and is seasoned with chili and turmeric. Some vendors make a hearty and tasty soup by adding a dash of regional herbs for a distinctive taste. It is available at a number of street food vendors and is particularly well liked in the winter months.

Thali Nagamese

Nagamese thali, a combo plate containing Nagaland delicacies such as smoked pork with bamboo shoots, rice, and local greens, is served by certain street sellers and small restaurants. These thalis provide a reasonably priced opportunity to experience Nagamese food, which is renowned for its strong, spicy tastes and distinctive cooking methods.

Coffee Stalls in the Himalayas

Even while Darjeeling is known for its tea, coffee shops are also growing in popularity, especially those that sell Himalayan coffee that is farmed nearby. Freshly brewed coffee is served at these stands, sometimes alongside regional fare like pastries or sel roti. The coffee is a pleasant substitute for tea because of its unique taste profile, which includes chocolate undertones and a smooth finish.

Jalebi and Samosa Stalls

In Darjeeling's marketplaces, samosa and jalebi stands are a regular sight for people in search of something sweet. While jalebis are spirals of dough dipped in sugar syrup and deep-fried, samosas are stuffed with spicy potatoes and peas. A local favorite, the combination of sweet jalebis and spicy samosas offers a pleasing blend of tastes.

Darjeeling provides a varied gastronomic experience, ranging from traditional delicacies steeped in cultural history to a thriving street food scene. Darjeeling's culinary culture, which reflects the town's history, customs, and friendly hospitality, is an integral element of every trip, whether it is enjoyed in a fancy restaurant, in a quaint café, or from street food vendors. Every meal and location provides a taste of Darjeeling's distinct fusion of tastes and culinary influences, creating lifelong memories for all foodies.

CHAPTER EIGHT: FESTIVALS AND EVENTS

Celebrations of Darjeeling's Cultural Heritage

The town's diverse mix of Bengali, Tibetan, Nepali, and Lepcha cultural influences is reflected in Darjeeling's festivals, which often bring together different ethnicities. Because of Darjeeling's uniqueness, every holiday is observed with distinctive customs, performances, and traditions that provide a window into the region's diverse cultural landscape.

Dasain (Dussehra)

One of the largest Hindu holidays observed by the Nepali people in Darjeeling is Dasain, also known as Dussehra. Dasain, a ten-day celebration that honors the goddess Durga, symbolizes the triumph of virtue over evil. In order to worship the goddess, people visit temples, clean and adorn their houses, and carry out rituals. Families get together to share presents and eat traditional meals, and elders bestow protection and prosperity on the younger members by blessing them with "tika," a crimson mark formed of grains and yogurt. Children and adults alike love kite-flying, a traditional Dasain hobby that fills Darjeeling's sky with vibrant kites.

Tibetan New Year, or Losar

For the Tibetan and Sherpa groups of Darjeeling, Losar is an important holiday. Based on the Tibetan lunar calendar, the Tibetan New Year is celebrated with colorful celebrations in February or March. Families start getting ready a week beforehand, cleaning their houses, making elaborate decorations, and cooking special meals. Darjeeling monasteries, like the Ghoom Monastery, celebrate the triumph of virtue over evil with prayer sessions and vibrant masked dances. Monks costumed as legendary animals and deities perform the dances, called cham. Families gather at Losar to celebrate with traditional cuisine, music, and prayer, as well as to give presents.

Sankranti Maghe

The Nepali community celebrates Maghe Sankranti, which signifies the end of winter and the start of the fortunate month of Magh. Celebrated on January 14th, it's a time for family get-togethers and eating. Special dishes are made for the event, such as "gundruk" (fermented leafy greens) and "sel roti," a traditional rice doughnut. Ritual baths in rivers are also taken by people in the belief that they will bless them and cleanse their souls. Families enjoy feasts, music, and traditional dances at Maghe Sankranti, which has a joyful mood.

Seasonal Festivals

Different seasonal festivals that align with harvests, blossoming seasons, and religious observances are made possible by Darjeeling's distinctive topography. The town's life is made more lively by seasonal events, which attract both residents and visitors.

Jayanti for Buddha

Buddha Jayanti, which is observed in April or May, honors Gautama Buddha's birth, enlightenment, and demise. Darjeeling celebrates Buddha Jayanti with awe and devotion as a hub for the Tibetan and Buddhist populations. Locals take part in prayer services, while temples and monasteries are decked up with flowers and prayer flags. Offerings of butter candles at monasteries, followed by monk-led prayers and chants, are among the most significant occasions. Both residents and pilgrims bring gifts and participate in meditation when they visit the Mahakal Temple and other Buddhist locations. Traditional dances and cultural events enhance the importance of this calm yet joyous occasion.

The Festival of Lights, or Tihar

One of the most colorful holidays in Darjeeling is Tihar, which is also called Deepavali in India. It is observed in October or November. Tihar, sometimes called the "festival of lights," is a five-day celebration that honors many animals of cultural importance in Nepal, such as oxen, cows, dogs, and crows. Oil lamps, candles, and vibrant rangolis—floor art created with flower petals, colored rice, and powder—are used to light homes and streets. Sisters conduct rituals for their brothers on the last day, "Bhai Tika," giving them wealth and a long life. Tihar is a stunning celebration that brings Darjeeling's streets to life with dancing, music, and lights.

The Festival of Colors, or Holi

Many groups in Darjeeling celebrate the lively and joyous celebration of Holi, which is usually held in March. Holi, also referred to as the "festival of colors," represents the coming of spring and the victory of good over evil. People congregate to play with colored powders and spray each other with vivid colors in public areas, temples, and private residences. The enthusiasm of the event is increased by traditional Holi songs and dances. Traditional music and dance, as well as delectable treats like "gujiya" (a fried pastry filled with a sweet concoction), are often included during Holi festivities in Darjeeling. Both residents and tourists participate in the celebration of colors and solidarity, creating a happy and friendly environment.

The Darjeeling Carnival

Usually celebrated in November, the Darjeeling Carnival is a contemporary event that highlights the town's rich musical and artistic traditions. The carnival, which is organized by neighborhood organizations, attempts to showcase the skills of local singers, artists, and entertainers while also promoting tourists. The carnival spans ten days and features street dances, live music acts, art exhibits, and food vendors serving regional specialties. Events take place all around town, with the Mall Road neighborhood acting as a focal point. The Darjeeling Carnival celebrates the town's distinctive history and contemporary inventiveness by bringing residents and visitors together in a joyous setting.

Unique Local Traditions

Beyond celebrations, Darjeeling boasts a number of distinctive regional traditions and customs that provide a richer understanding of the town's cultural makeup. The diversity of ethnic communities, each with its own customs and beliefs, frequently influences these practices.

Puja Bhimsen

The Newar community in Darjeeling observes a distinctive local custom called Bhimsen Puja. The Newars worship Bhimsen, a deity linked to strength and trade, because they think he provides the community with protection and prosperity. Families come together to participate in prayers and rituals, and offerings of fruits, flowers, and traditional foods are made to the deity. This yearly puja is a time for family and friends to gather in gratitude and is frequently celebrated with a feast.

Harvest Dance, or Dhan Naach

The Dhan Naach, or "harvest dance," is a celebration of the harvest season among the Lepcha and Rai communities in Darjeeling. In order to give thanks to the earth for a good harvest and to ask for blessings for the next planting season, this traditional dance is performed. Traditional instruments like the madal (a drum), vibrant clothing, and rhythmic motions are all part of the dance. People from the community congregate in open spaces to celebrate with food, dancing, and singing. The Dhan Naach, which symbolizes the bond between the people and their land, is a sign of appreciation and a vital aspect of Darjeeling rural life.

Dance of Chyabrung

The Chyabrung Dance is a significant aspect of the Limbu community's cultural expression in Darjeeling. It is a vibrant performance that comprises dancers banging chyabrung (a traditional double-headed drum) in rhythmic patterns while dancing in a circular shape. Performed at festivals and social events, the dance signifies peace and togetherness. Dancers wear bright costumes and dance in rhythm with the beat of the drums, creating a stunning visual and audio experience. This dance is not just a source of entertainment but also a method for the Limbu people to retain and express their cultural identity.

Chaita Dasain

Chaita Dasain, separate from the major Dasain celebration in October, is held in the Nepali month of Chaitra (March or April). It's a smaller version of Dasain and features similar customs, including worshiping Durga and getting blessings from elders. Unlike the major Dasain, Chaita Dasain is more localized and mostly followed by the elder generation, who execute ancient rituals to safeguard the family from bad spirits. This event provides an occasion for individuals to pay tribute to their ancestors, and it's a time for quiet introspection rather than large-scale festivities.

Traditional Wedding Ceremonies

Traditional wedding celebrations in Darjeeling, especially among the Nepali, Tibetan, and Lepcha groups, are a colorful cultural event. Weddings are generally extravagant and may run for many days, featuring ceremonies, dances, and music. In Nepali weddings, for example, the bride and groom exchange garlands, and the ritual incorporates a number of traditions such as "swayamvar," which is the self-choice of a spouse, and "kanyadaan," which is the giving away of the bride. At Tibetan marriages, butter tea and barley wine are offered together with lama chanting. These marriages provide a window into the social mores and ingrained beliefs of the cultures.

By fusing spirituality, seasonal cycles, and community bonds, Darjeeling's festivals and distinctive local customs weave a vibrant tapestry of cultural diversity. Darjeeling's traditions showcase its warmth and variety, ranging from well-known festivals like Dasain and Losar to lesser-known practices like Bhimsen Puja and Chaita Dasain. Travelers may enjoy the peaceful cohabitation of many ethnic groups that contribute to Darjeeling's distinctiveness and cultural diversity by attending these events, which provide an immersive cultural experience.

CHAPTER NINE: SHOPPING AND SOUVENIRS

Famous Markets and Bazaars

With its vibrant marketplaces and bazaars, Darjeeling provides a varied shopping experience where you can buy anything from fresh local goods to traditional handicrafts. These marketplaces, which sell goods exclusive to Darjeeling and the surrounding districts, are a reflection of the region's cultural legacy.

Mall Road

The center of Darjeeling's retail scene is Mall Road, often referred to as Chowrasta. Shops offering a variety of souvenirs, handicrafts, wool clothing, and Tibetan antiquities fill this pedestrian-only neighborhood. Mall Road is particularly well-known for its bookstores, which have a wide range of publications about the Himalayan area, including history books, guides, and novels written by local writers. Mall Road is a well-liked location for travelers to relax since it provides expansive views of the Kanchenjunga mountain in addition to shopping.

Road Nehru

Nehru Road, which is close to Mall Road, is home to a diverse array of stores and street sellers. This neighborhood, which is well-known for its lively ambiance, has stores that offer textiles, handicrafts, and Darjeeling tea. Here, one may often find handcrafted bags, woolen shawls, and Tibetan carpets. This is one of the greatest sites to get genuine, high-quality Darjeeling tea. Tea-tasting sessions are offered by several stores here, so you may sample various types before buying.

Market of Bhutan

Locals and visitors alike frequent Bhutia Market for reasonably priced winter apparel. The market, which is mostly run by Tibetan sellers, sells a variety of woolen products manufactured by regional craftspeople, including scarves, gloves, sweaters, and hats. The rates are reasonable, and the woolen products are of great quality. Bhutia Market is a great place to get one-of-a-kind gifts since it is also well-known for traditional Tibetan jewelry and trinkets.

Market at Ghoom Monastery

You may discover traditional Tibetan handicrafts, prayer flags, and Thangka paintings at this little market, which is close to the well-known Ghoom Monastery. It is a well-liked destination for those with a spiritual bent since vendors here also offer religious goods, including incense, prayer wheels, and beads. The market offers a tranquil shopping experience away from the bustle of Darjeeling town thanks to its serene surroundings and the monastery's presence.

The Haat Bazaar

Every Wednesday and Saturday, farmers from nearby villages bring fresh vegetables, dairy products, and handcrafted goods to the weekly Haat Bazaar. Local fruits, including oranges and plums, as well as handcrafted jams, honey, and pickles, are all available here. Fresh and organic items from local farmers may be found at this market, which also provides a window into the rural way of life in the area.

Handicrafts and Artisanal Products

The multi-ethnic culture of the area has inspired the handicrafts of Darjeeling, which include Tibetan, Nepali, and Indian crafts. Local craftspeople are skilled in producing one-of-a-kind items that serve as genuine and significant mementos.

Tibetan Rugs and Carpets

Tibetan carpets, renowned for their elaborate patterns and long-lasting quality, are among the most sought-after things in Darjeeling. These hand-knotted carpets are made from premium wool and include traditional Tibetan designs, including dragons, flowers, and wealth symbols. The carpets are an investment in both art and functionality, and they are available in a variety of sizes. For finding genuine Tibetan carpets, stores around the Tibetan Refugee Center and Bhutia Market are well liked.

Paintings by Thangka

Traditional Tibetan artworks known as Thangka paintings are made on silk or cotton. These paintings, which are used as meditation and religious aids, include mandalas, deities, and scenes from Buddhist mythology. These intricate, colorful paintings are made by talented Darjeeling craftsmen and might take weeks or even months to finish. Those with an interest in Buddhist culture will find thangkas to be an excellent memento. They may be found in stores close to monasteries, such as the Ghoom Monastery Market.

Handcrafted Paper Goods

Notebooks, diaries, and greeting cards are among the handcrafted paper goods manufactured by Darjeeling artisans. Natural fibers and recyclable garbage are among the locally sourced resources used to create these eco-friendly items. Natural textures and distinctive patterns, such as embossed patterns or pressed flowers, are often seen in the handmade paper goods. These things are inexpensive and portable, making them convenient to bring home as presents.

Scarves & Shawls Made of Wool

Purchase woolen goods in Darjeeling, including sweaters, scarves, and shawls that are handknitted. The premium wool used to make the woolen goods at Bhutia Market and Haat Bazaar is produced by regional craftspeople who are proficient in age-old weaving methods. They are perfect for warmth and elegance because of their vivid hues and designs. Additionally, community-owned stores that support local craftsmen sell woolen goods made locally.

Tea Items

Tea from Darjeeling is well known across the globe, and a trip to the region wouldn't be complete without acquiring this cherished item. With their unique tastes, First Flush, Second Flush, and Autumn Flush are the greatest types. Premium, single-origin Darjeeling teas are available at several shops along Mall Road and Nehru Road. Tea-related souvenirs, including handcrafted teacups and strainers, are also available in certain stores and make excellent presents.

Tibetan Jewels

In Darjeeling, Tibetan jewelry—which is often made of silver and semi-precious stones—is quite popular. Traditional patterns and spiritual symbols, such as the Om sign, lotus flower, or mantra inscriptions, are used to embellish items like pendants, rings, and bracelets. These goods are lovely, culturally significant mementos and may be found in marketplaces such as the Bhutia Market and the Ghoom Monastery Market.

Tips for Shopping in Darjeeling

A few pointers will help you get the most out of your Darjeeling shopping experience. Your visit to the town's markets and bazaars will be improved by haggling, comprehending the authenticity of the products, and knowing where to find local specialties.

Deal Sensibly

Bargaining is a common practice in most markets, particularly Bhutia Market and Haat Bazaar. Vendors anticipate price haggling from their clients, and courteous, respectful haggling frequently results in a better bargain. However, since artisanal and handmade goods take a lot of time and skill to produce, try not to haggle too much over them.

Select Genuine Tea Suppliers

Seek out trustworthy stores that provide authenticity certification while purchasing Darjeeling tea. Information on the tea flush (harvest season), which influences the taste, and the estate where the tea was produced are often available at local retailers. Ask for a tea sampling if you're not sure which kind will work best for you. To guarantee quality, stay away from purchasing tea from unlicensed street sellers.

Purchase from locally owned stores

The Tibetan refugee population and local craftspeople are supported by a number of community-owned businesses and cooperatives in Darjeeling. These stores provide genuine handicrafts, often at affordable costs, and the proceeds go straight to helping out local artisans. In addition to ensuring quality, shopping at these stores supports the local economy.

Mind the Season for Woolen Goods

If you're wanting to purchase woolen products like scarves, gloves, and sweaters, come during the winter months (October to February) when dealers stock new designs. During this period, you'll discover a broader choice of brands and designs, guaranteeing that you obtain high-quality, warm things.

Respect Cultural Symbols

When acquiring goods with religious or cultural importance, such as Thangka paintings or prayer flags, it's crucial to manage them appropriately. Avoid putting these things on the ground or in improper situations, since they frequently possess great cultural and religious importance. This regard enriches your experience and makes a great impression on local sellers.

Examine handmade items closely.

To guarantee quality, thoroughly scrutinize any handcrafted goods you purchase, particularly jewelry and paper goods. For handcrafted works in particular, pay attention to features like authenticity, durability, and finishing. In general, Darjeeling vendors are willing to let clients examine products carefully before making a purchase.

Keep cash on hand.

Many smaller vendors and marketplaces still use cash, even if some stores on Mall Road and Nehru Road could take digital payments. Keep adequate small-denomination currency on hand since merchants often have little change. Although there are often ATMs close to the major markets, it's a good idea to pack extra cash to prevent any hassles.

Darjeeling shopping offers more than simply mementos; it's a window into the town's tradition, cultural diversity, and handcrafted workmanship. Every shopping experience offers a glimpse into the heart of Darjeeling, from the busy shops of Mall Road to the serene nooks of Ghoom Monastery Market. Visitors may depart Darjeeling with souvenirs that perfectly capture the allure and genuineness of this mountain town thanks to distinctive handicrafts, traditional goods, and local buying advice.

CHAPTER TEN:
CONCLUSION

Key Takeaways from Darjeeling

High in the Himalayas, Darjeeling is a veritable gold mine of scenic beauty, rich cultural history, and enjoyable activities. A few important lessons will enhance your trip, regardless of whether you are attracted to it by its breathtaking mountain vistas, famous tea, or lively local culture:

1. Gorgeous Landscapes: The highlights of every journey to Darjeeling are the mesmerizing vistas of the Kanchenjunga mountain and verdant valleys. The many hiking routes give different viewpoints of this breathtaking terrain, and early mornings spent watching the dawn from Tiger Hill offer a dreamlike experience.

2. Rich Cultural Heritage: Tibetan, Nepali, and British colonial histories have all had a significant effect on the town, which is a cultural melting pot. The festivals, food, and architecture all reflect this. While interacting with local populations highlights the region's varied customs, seeing nearby temples and monasteries illustrates the spiritual side of Darjeeling life.

3. Renowned Tea Culture: Darjeeling is known for its superior tea. The painstaking process of growing and producing tea may be understood by visiting the tea estates. You may get a deeper appreciation for this well-known beverage by participating in tea tastings and learning about the many variations.

4. Adventure and Nature: Darjeeling provides plenty of chances for adventure in addition to leisure. The area offers activities for both thrill-seekers and environment lovers, such as mountain biking, paragliding, and hiking in the Himalayas. Your relationship with nature is strengthened as you explore the varied flora and animals at locations like Padmaja Naidu Himalayan Zoological Park.

5. Dynamic Local Markets: Darjeeling's markets are hives of activity where you may discover regional products, handicrafts, and antiques. You may carry a little of this magical place home with you when you shop for Tibetan jewelry, handcrafted wool clothing, and genuine Darjeeling tea.

6. Culinary Delights: Darjeeling's cuisine showcases the region's diverse cultural heritage. The local food is a blend of tastes worth trying, from Tibetan thukpa to traditional Nepali dumplings (momos). In addition to satisfying your palette, dining in neighborhood cafés and restaurants allows you to experience the local cuisine.

7. Festivals & Celebrations: Taking part in regional celebrations like Dashain, Tihar, and the Darjeeling Carnival provides an insight into the rich customs and sense of community of the area. By taking part in these festivities, you may make lifelong memories and enrich your cultural experience.

Final Tips for Travelers

Take into account the following advice to guarantee a satisfying trip to Darjeeling:

1. Create your itinerary: Considering the variety of sights and things to do, creating your itinerary is essential. Incorporate must-see locations such as tea farms, the Darjeeling Himalayan Railway, and Tiger Hill. But make room for impromptu travel and cross-cultural interactions.

2. Acclimatization: Due to Darjeeling's high elevation, it is essential to adequately acclimate in order to prevent altitude sickness. Your first day should be spent unwinding and progressively increasing your level of exercise. Pay attention to your body and stay hydrated.

3. Wear layers: Darjeeling has chilly mornings and nights, and the weather may change quickly. Wearing layers makes it easier to adjust to changes in temperature. During the rainy season, don't forget to pack necessities like a raincoat or umbrella, comfortable walking shoes, and a warm jacket.

4. Respect Local Customs: It's important to keep in mind regional traditions and customs. Learn a few simple words in Nepali or Tibetan to establish a connection with the people, dress modestly while visiting places of worship, and get permission before taking pictures of them.

5. Stay Connected: Having a local SIM card might improve your experience, even if access can be erratic in certain places. It lets you communicate with other travelers, utilize maps, and post about your travels on social media. Find out which network providers in the area have the greatest coverage.

6. Local Transportation: Learn about the famous Darjeeling Himalayan Railway, taxis, and shared jeeps, as well as other local modes of transportation. By providing a window into locals' everyday lives, public transportation may improve your trip.

7. Health Precautions: Since pharmacies may not carry everything, bring along any prescription drugs you may need. To prevent stomach problems, use purification pills or bottled water instead of tap water.

8. Talk to Locals: You may make your trip more enjoyable by interacting with locals. These relationships, whether by exchanging tales or studying the skills of store owners, often result in original ideas and suggestions for undiscovered treasures.

9. Be Ready for Weather Changes: Especially during the monsoon season (June to September), the weather might change suddenly. Keep an eye on the weather and be ready for unexpected rainstorms or temperature swings.

10. Leave No Trace: It's critical for tourists to engage in sustainable tourism. Refrain from polluting, show consideration for animals, and patronize nearby businesses. By doing this, you favorably impact the conservation of Darjeeling's natural splendor and cultural authenticity.

Making Lasting Memories

Immersion in Darjeeling's natural beauty and lively culture is key to making lifelong memories there. The following ideas can help you have a better experience:

1. Seize the experiences: Remember to pack a camera so you may document the breathtaking scenery, lively marketplaces, and special experiences. But while taking pictures of residents and their houses, keep in mind to show them respect. Request permission, particularly in areas that are sensitive to cultural differences.

2. Take Part in Cultural Experiences: To get a deeper understanding of the culture, take part in local programs like tea tastings or handicraft displays. These encounters shed light on the customs and abilities of the local populace.

3. Discover Off the Beaten Path: Although well-known sites are unmissable, think about visiting lesser-known locales. To see Darjeeling's more subdued side, visit remote monasteries, undiscovered vistas, and nearby villages. These locations often provide isolation and tranquility away from throngs of tourists.

4. Maintain a travel diary: Write down your observations, ideas, and experiences in a travel diary. You may revisit memories and record your thoughts of the people, places, and events that speak to you by writing about your voyage.

5. Experience Local Flavors: Make it a point to try a range of street food and regional cuisine. Every culinary encounter helps you learn more about the local way of life, whether you're eating momos from a street seller or drinking freshly made Darjeeling tea.

6. Spend Time with Locals: Interacting with locals might result in memorable encounters.

Engage in dialogue, inquire about their lives, and discover their customs. These exchanges often result in suggestions for undiscovered locations and provide a more genuine travel experience.

7. Make a Photo Album: After your journey, put together a collection of pictures from your Darjeeling experience. You may retain the tales and memories connected to your experiences by adding notes and descriptions to each picture.

8. Tell About Your Experiences: When you go back home, tell your friends and family about your adventures in Darjeeling. This encourages others to discover this captivating location in addition to allowing you to relive the experiences.

9. Keep in contact: If you've developed relationships with locals, think about staying in contact via letters or social media. Expressing thanks and providing life updates may build enduring connections that cut across geographic borders.

10. Reflect on Your Journey: After your journey, spend some time thinking back on the things you've discovered and gone through. Think about the effects the trip has had on you and how it could affect your future trips. Your appreciation for the locations you visit and the people you encounter may grow as a result of this contemplation.

Everyone who visits Darjeeling is left with a lasting impression of this amazing place. It provides experiences that linger long after the trip is over because of its breathtaking landscapes, diverse cultural heritage, and kind people. Following these suggestions and embracing the area's distinctive features can help you make lifelong experiences that will motivate you to visit again.

SAFE JOURNEYS!!!

Printed in Dunstable, United Kingdom